MW01123031

Linda Crowley

In Praise of *Me, Ruby, and God*

"*Me, Ruby, and God* is a delightful, heartwarming, inspirational book. Linda Crowley has a wonderful way of expressing her innermost feelings and impressions on life through her relationships with her dogs, most especially Ruby. I was able to relate to many of her experiences and gleaned helpful spiritual lessons. I laughed, cried, and had my heart wonderfully warmed. At times, I couldn't put the book down. I highly recommend this book to anyone who seeks to draw closer to God, especially those who know the wonder of sharing their lives with beloved pets."

- **Nancy Kratz Offen,** *author of Step, Hobble Step*

"*Me, Ruby, and God* came to me at a time I was feeling down, and self-centered. This is one of the most powerful books I have read in some time. The power of God to heal and see you through is all encompassing. As a fellow musher, I also see signs from God through my sled dogs. Wonderful and well done!"

- **Debra Su Stevens,** *Colorado Mountain Mushers*

"I would recommend this book to anyone who wants or needs to grow in Christ."

- **Rev. Peter Bush,** *Taylor Wesleyan Church*

ME, RUBY, AND GOD

A JOURNAL OF
SPIRITUAL GROWTH

ME, RUBY, AND GOD

A JOURNAL OF SPIRITUAL GROWTH

Linda Crowley

Illustrations by Margi Greene

Golden Ruby Publishing
Cincinnatus, New York

Golden Ruby Publishing
3822 Taylor Valley Road
Cincinnatus, New York 13040
www.GoldenRuby.com

Cover Design by Suzette Vaughn
Illustrations by Margi Greene
Designed and formatted by Cassandra Bowen, Uzuri Designs

Ordering Information:
Special discounts are available on quantity purchases by churches, corporations,
associations, and others. For details, contact the "Special Sales Department" at
the address above.

Me, Ruby, and God – Author Linda Crowley, 1st ed.

Dedication

This book is dedicated to my beloved husband who first introduced me to God, and then supported and encouraged me throughout the long writing process and, of course, to Ruby. To most, she is just another non-descript Siberian Husky sled dog, but for me, she will always be God's messenger.

Acknowledgements

Special thanks to my daughter, Tiffany, whose own efforts to write and publish her book has inspired me to push myself to publish this work, and to my editor from FaithWriters.com,
Shann Hall-LochmannVanBennekom,
who taught me so much and helped
me improve my writing.

CONTENTS

PROLOGUE

I run sled dogs. That statement alone is enough to demonstrate my insanity. Unlike most mushers, I choose to race Siberian Huskies instead of a faster breed, putting an emphasis on running, rather than racing. But being considered odd is so common that it has become a part of who I am. Perhaps that is why the strange conceptions that have unfolded through Ruby are easy to place as another eccentricity.

After a clandestine one-night stand, my young lead dog surprised me with a litter of two. I was determined to keep one of the pups and selected the little red girl. I named her Ruby after the town on the Iditarod Trail. Little did I know how much this crazy pup would change my life.

The first couple of years went by without incident. I was absorbed in my dogs and was happily living what I thought was a Christian life. For the most part, I ignored God, except on Sunday mornings when I wasn't running a race. For my part, I was pretty well convinced that He was ignoring me. God must have been tired of my indifference and had to slap me up the side of the head to get my attention. Ruby was the four-footed brickbat he used.

I Believe

I believe in angels…as long as the TV is playing.
I believe in ghosts…at least while the movie is showing.
I believe in hobbits, while I read Tolkien.
And I believe in God, the Almighty Father,
In Jesus, his only begotten Son,
And in the Holy Spirit…
At least on Sundays.

I am uncomfortable with my shallow belief.
My religion should be at a deeper level than
Harry Potter's wizardry. I should believe with all
my heart and soul.
It should affect every waking moment of my life.
I could not live my life the way I do now
If I truly believed.

I believe in sunshine, even at night.
I believe in stars, even when I can't see them.
Why do I have such a hard time believing in eternal life?
Why do I put boundaries on God?
Why is the Resurrection so difficult for me to conceive?
Why is my faith so weak?
Help me, Lord, with my unbelief.

Amen.

CHAPTER ONE

Stigmata

One frosty April morning, the barking and fussing in the kennel rouses me from my sleep. *Perhaps there is a deer or fox near the fence causing the excitement,* I mentally mumble. Crawling from beneath the covers, I begin to dress. I pull on my blue jeans and start to reach for an old yellow T-shirt when my husband points out that the dogs are still yipping. Yawning, I step into my worn leather moccasins and scuffle to the balcony to look. From my vantage point, I can see out the upper windows, past the yard, to the two large kennel pens backed against the tree line, where my team lives. The dogs are crazed with excitement. It isn't a wild animal disturbing them, however, but a dogfight. The four girls in the front pen are engaged in an argument that is rapidly escalating from circling and verbal threats to snapping and slashing with an apparent intent to maim or destroy each other. Without intervention, there will be serious bloodshed.

Instantly awake, I race down the stairs. Time is of the essence, and I don't waste any precious seconds grabbing more clothes. At least I don't have any neighbors to see me flying out the door in just jeans and a bra. Slipping and sliding, I run down the path to the kennel, shaking off my slippers for better traction on the half-frozen ice. My bare feet sink up to my ankles in the icy, gravelly mud and frigid rain is pouring down, but these are only inconveniences. The life of a dog is at stake, and I must hurry.

As I approach, I can see the three older girls circling and looking for an opening as Ruby spins around to face them with bared teeth and defiance in her eyes. The dispute erupts into action as Gale launches herself at Ruby, grabbing her by the scruff of the neck and shaking her. Frantic, Ruby tries to pull away, but Abbey and Beth shoulder in, grabbing a foreleg and an ear as they knock her down. Gale lets off her hold on the neck and growls for Ruby to submit. But my foolish girl won't give in so easily. Leaping to her feet, she catches Gale under the chin and forces her up and back. Gale twists away and circles around. Beth snakes her head in for another ear grab while Abbey yanks at her tail. As Gale charges in again, they all go down in a snarl of flying fur and snapping teeth.

It seems to take forever to get the gate unchained. In vain, I'm screaming at the dogs the entire time, trying to get their attention and get them to break off their attack. "No! Stop it! Girls—no! Break it up!" At last, the gate swings open, and I step into the melee, trying to figure out my best approach. Ruby is still alive and fighting back. I grab Beth as she breaks loose to circle around again, seeking a fresh grip, and I push her out the gate. Abbey still has Ruby's blonde tail clenched in her teeth and doesn't want to let go. With

one hand on the collar and another on her tail, I grapple Abbey away from the battle. Freed from one attacker, Ruby, still on her back, lunges at Abbey as I move her away. She misses her opponent and clamps down on my bare ankle instead. Immediately, Ruby realizes her mistake, rolls her eyes at me, and then releases my leg. *Thank God, she didn't tear my ankle open,* I think. Abbey bounces stiff-legged, trying to twist back to the battle as I shove her out the gate where my husband is waiting to help. His calm presence gives me the strength I need to return to the fight. Gratefully, I catch the heavy down parka he flips over the fence for me; not only will it keep me warmer, but it will provide a bit more protection to my body should someone go for an intruding arm.

With the first two aggressors shut away, my husband joins me in the pen where Gale and Ruby are still locked in combat. Between the two of us, we separate the dogs. Ruby staggers to her feet and looks around. She has a small cut on her foreleg and a slight tear on one ear but no obvious heavy bleeding. She'll have to come inside for a more thorough exam, so I go back to the house for a leash. I take the time to grab some socks and boots. My feet are numb with cold and scraped from the ice and gravel. We bring Ruby into the house and crate her. Right now, she needs warmth and quiet to avoid shock. I go back out, rearrange the dogs, and give them their breakfast to get their minds off the fight.

By the time I'm done with the chores, it's apparent that something is very wrong with my leg—every step is agony. I limp back into the house to check it out. My lower leg is swollen to near twice normal and has an ugly black and blue patch the size of my palm. In the center are a couple of puncture marks. Not only has Ruby's bite broken the skin, but she also has savaged the tissue.

Three months roll by, and the injury remains ugly looking. I have seen the doctor several times, swallowed my share of antibiotics, and suffered innumerable medications. Still, it will not heal. The doctors have decided that a more drastic measure is necessary in order to stop the flesh-eating decay and save my leg. I am scheduled for surgery to remove a patch of skin from my thigh and graft it over the wound. The doctors aren't sure that even that will turn things around.

In the hospital, the pungent smell of disinfectant oppresses me as I lay on the bed, waiting for the anesthesiologists. The warmth of the blanket doesn't reach into my shivering heart. A nurse in colorful scrubs—a bright contrast to the sterile whites surrounding me—carefully tucks my waist-length braid into a paper cap. She then directs my husband to leave. He gives my hand a squeeze, tucks stray wisps of silver-streaked dark hair back under the blue cap, and with a quick farewell kiss assures me I will be fine. I have plenty of time to think. I consider what I've done, the risks involved, and the consequences of my actions.

Little did I realize that when I jumped into the fray that the act of saving Ruby would jeopardize my own health. But even knowing that I would be hurt like this, I still would have done it. There is no way Ruby would have survived if I hadn't intervened. Thoughts run through my mind as I try to make sense of it all. *If I knew I might lose my leg, would I still have jumped in to save my dog? Yes, I would. Dog people know they must take risks for their dogs. But what if the risks were even greater—what if I knew my very life was endangered; what would I have done then?* The "what-if's" continue to haunt me. *What if I knew it would cost me my life? I know of a few people who have laid down their lives trying to save their dogs. Would I still do the same? It would be different if Ruby were a human. Surely, I would be quicker to sacrifice my future if I were saving someone's life.* At least I like to think I would have done so.

Ruby dear, I hope you're worth it! Almost immediately, I laugh at my thoughts, as if a mere dog could understand the price that I would pay. Now if it were a person being saved, I might expect some kind of life-change, some show of gratitude. But not with a dog; they don't think the way people do. If I had saved a human, it would be different. *What would I expect in return? Turn the tables—if I was the one being saved, how would that change me? What would I do differently if someone saved me?*

The sobering reality suddenly hits me. Someone did lay down His life for me. I have been saved from death, from eternal death. What have I done to show my gratitude? All this time purporting to be a Christian, I have claimed, "I believe," but I haven't been living it. Instead, I've been living in a self-centered reality of my own creation. I haven't bothered even to thank my Savior. Suddenly I don't like myself very much.

I come out of surgery, grateful to be alive and still have two legs. Ruby may not be worth it as a sled dog; she may not show me any more gratitude or respect than the other dogs do, but I am grateful for her. She has shown me something about my relationship with God. With luck, the scar on my leg will remain; it is my stigmata, a constant reminder to me of God's great sacrifice.

A Prayer for Healing

Lord, a scar is a sign of a past injury.
I have been injured; now the healing has begun.
You have allowed this scar
So that I may always remember
What You have done for others,
What You have done for me.
When I see this, my scar,
A remembrance of what has happened,
Let me never forget You, never doubt You,
But always believe in You.
Though my eyes may look upon disfigurement,
Let me see beyond it.
Let me see the inner beauty of the soul,
Not just surface appearances.
Lord, thank You for this mark You have placed on me.
Thank You for the healing You have offered me.
Teach me, O Lord, to use it wisely.

Amen.

CHAPTER TWO

Spiritual Showers

It's April again. This time of year, as the snow melts and the spring rain drizzles for days at a time, the kennel yard is a sea of slippery, brown mud that reeks of decaying straw and dog droppings. Exuberant to greet me each morning, the dogs leap against the fence and fling the muddy water all over me. Ruby is possibly the worst offender. With her abundance of high energy, she is an exceptionally bouncy dog. In addition, a large puddle of odorous water insists on establishing itself under her gate. As I approach her pen, she leaps at the fence. Her exuberant greeting leaves me drenched. There is little doubt that I will need a shower before I go to work.

Back in the house, I shed the first layer of clothes. Hat, coat, boots, and wind pants all are wet with the muddy water. The damp has permeated to my shirt, pants, and even my underwear. In the shower, as I watch the water stream off me, rinsing away the first layer of dirt, I recall with a chuckle of amusement a childhood incident.

It was just after Easter and we were having hard-boiled eggs again. My mother told me to wash up for lunch.

I dutifully trotted off to the bathroom and gave my hands a cursory rinse under the faucet before returning to the table.

"Did you wash?" my mother asked.

I glanced at my hands, checking to see if I had missed something obvious to provoke that question. They appeared clean. "Yes." I picked up a pretty egg dyed a light blue and rapped it on the counter to crack the shell. I began to pick off the colorful pieces but to my dismay, the moisture on the egg turned muddy as my hands made contact with its fresh cleanness. I don't know if I was more worried about the dirty egg or my mother's frown. I so wanted to please her and help in the kitchen. "I washed my hands!" I cried, "Honest, I did!"

"Go clean them again. And use soap!" she ordered.

I went back to the bathroom and washed, this time with soap and water. I looked them over before I returned to the table. Surely, they were clean now. But once again, the eggs revealed the awful truth—there was still dirt on my hands, even though I hadn't seen it. One more scrubbing, this time I reached all the usually ignored places; at last, my hands were clean enough for my mother to allow me to proceed.

In the shower, soap, water, and plenty of scrubbing are the order of the morning. I am going to work and must be clean and fresh. I squeeze the lilac-scented body wash on the nylon-net scrubby and work the suds across my front, under my arms, and down my legs. It's funny how our modern society has put so much emphasis on being clean. I look at the shower shelf where a variety of soaps and shampoos reside, far more than two people really need. I'm just as guilty of overdoing it as anyone. After I've scrubbed and cleaned, I treat myself with deodorant and breath-freshener, striving to keep any remnant of human odor from my body. On top of that, I add perfumed lotion to further disguise my natural scent. It's as if I have become phobic of the dirt and sweat that previously had marked a hardworking person. I fear our society places too much money and attention on common dirt and places value on cleanliness only at a surface level.

When Ruby and her companions splash me with mud, coat me with their hair, and cover me with their doggie kisses, I feel I need to clean myself before going out in public. I would hate to smell of dirt and dogs at work, but what about the malodor of sin? Do I reek of spiritual filth? I look at myself and think, I'm not a bad person. I'm not stained with sin. What do I have to worry about? Then I recall the Easter eggs and the dirt that was hidden from my eye. I think sin must be a lot like that. While I don't think I'm covered in filth, perhaps the eyes of God see otherwise. How accepting of me can He be if I am not cleansed?

I consider the fresh purity of the Risen Christ and begin to see myself as I am. Because of my physically close relationship with other people, I insist on a daily shower. It follows that if I want close companionship with God, I should pay equal attention to my spiritual cleanliness. Perhaps I should strive for a daily "spiritual shower" to wash away the stains of sin that I have overlooked and to prepare myself for

a new day close to God. Ruby may not care about the many layers of cleanliness, but others, like God and me, do care. I consider what a daily spiritual shower would consist of.
I think I'll begin mine with a prayer.

A Prayer for Cleansing

Wash me clean, O Lord!
Cleanse me of my sins,
My failings, my weaknesses.
Open my eyes so that I can see where I have failed.
Teach me how to become better, more like You
So that I don't hurt You anymore.
You are gentle and forgiving in Your love.
Teach me Your ways.
I love You, my Lord,
And I don't want to hurt You again.
I don't want to soil You anymore.
Forgive me, and give me a fresh start.
Wash me clean.

Amen.

CHAPTER THREE

Crying

Another day in the kennel and the air is heavy with the threat of still more rain. The dogs are restless. They pace back and forth, pushing and shoving as they compete for my attention. I open the chain link gate and go into the pen Ruby shares with Flash and Corrie to feed and clean up. With an exuberance that doesn't match the dull sky, Ruby nearly knocks her food pan out of my hand, while Flash jumps up and jabs me in tender places with his rough paws. Not wanting to be left out, Corrie leaps to the top of the doghouse so she can snatch my red knit hat from my head as I walk by. They aren't showing any appreciation for my care, only their selfish greed. I slip in the mud and manage to trip in one of the numerous holes they have dug, wrenching my ankle. I snag my favorite sweatshirt—the teal one with

Iditarod printed on it—on a protruding wire as I try to slip back out the gate. It's a tight squeeze since one of the hinges is broken and doesn't let it properly open. "Why doesn't my husband get out here and fix the gate?" I mutter, "It isn't fair. Why should I be the only one taking care of these dogs"?

Frustrated and discouraged, I begin to question myself. *Why should I, with my college degree and such a promising future, be reduced to merely an attendant for a pack of ungrateful huskies? Why should I be scraping up dog dirt day after day, while other people don't seem to have such menial demands on their time? They make money, indulge in their passions, and have fun. Where did I go wrong?*

I look up in despair at the gray skies and mentally shake a fist at a god who let me down. Suddenly, the heavenly taps open and rain begins to fall—it's as if the tears of the Father are mingling with my own. Could God actually be crying for me? *Surely not, for I'm just one more nobody in this big world.* I shake my head in continued disbelief and turn back to my chores. *The heavenly Father can't care about me.*

The dogs have finished eating, and it's time for me to gather up their pans. Ruby must sense that I'm still upset. Laying her ears back, she gives her tail a tentative wag, then comes over and offers me gentle kisses. I return her caress as I ruffle her red-furred ears with my hand. She doesn't care if I have a college degree or if I had a promising future as a teen. She just loves me because I'm me, who I am today. The fact that I spend my days caring for her just makes her life easier. That may be what God is asking of me now, to make life good for my dogs, His creatures. I recall that I dedicated the dogs to him several years ago when I began this mushing venture. So why should I complain and feel sorry for myself now? I've been moaning that Ruby doesn't fully appreciate the sacrifices I make for her and the other dogs, yet can I honestly say that I have fully appreciated what God has done for me?

Ruby may resent the collar I have put on her. She probably feels the fencing I installed to keep her safe hinders her freedom. But she doesn't see the entire picture. Neither do I. I can't see the entire picture of God's plan for my life. At times, I feel abandoned, unloved, and undeserving of my fate. I wallow in self-pity just as I am now wallowing in the mud of the dog yard. I want God's undivided attention, just as Ruby begs for mine. I want Him to explain to me what He wants of me, and I want him to provide generously for me in a way that I can more feel more easily. I want...I want...I want. Oh, selfish soul of mine, no wonder God is crying for me! It is at this moment that I realize that God really does care for me as an individual.

Lord, here I am, standing alone with just our dogs in the mud of the dog yard. I understand Your tears better now. I will try to accept my place here. I look up to the heavens and welcome the rain as it flows down my face. In awe of God's goodness, I kneel in the mud and let His holy tears begin to cleanse me. Lord, would You please wash me clean and help me to start over? I need to focus on Your desires, not my dreams. Will You remake my spirit and leave out the selfishness?

A Prayer for a New Beginning

Lord, You know that I need to start over.
I have failed in so many ways;
I just don't have the foundation I need.
My only hope is to start over, with You as my foundation.
I say this every week, every day,
but somehow I always make the same mistakes.
As long as I am just me, trying to do it by myself,
I think I will have problems.
I need to start over. Every day I need to start over.
Help me to see that each day IS a new day,
and that I don't have to tackle life alone.
You are with me. You are available to be my foundation;
I just need to ask.
So, dear Lord, I am asking You now.
Help me, please, help me again to begin anew.

Amen.

CHAPTER FOUR

Like Siberians, We Have All Gone Astray

Ruby has run off. She was safe in her pen with Corrie, but at some point, the two of them decided to stage a breakout, and despite the pouring rain, they have taken off. After eleven PM, Bob goes out to give the housedogs a last potty break and discovers Corrie running loose. Corrie comes happily into the house, but Ruby is nowhere to be found. Ruby has always been one to circle around and make for the house door, to have taken off in the rain at night doesn't make a lot of sense. But she is gone. Surely, I think, she will return in the morning. *She will hear the others doing their morning howl, and a rumbling stomach will remind her that it is breakfast time.*

The next morning, the rain stops, and the sun peeks out from behind the empty clouds. I think, *Little girl, it's a good time to come out of wherever you have holed up.* Yet, still, there is no Ruby. I feed the dogs and call her name repeatedly. There is no answer, no excited yaps as she bounces up to greet me. My heart sinks. Bob and I drive around and look for her; I watch out my window, searching for a glimpse of her strawberry blonde flashing in the tree line, but she isn't to be seen. *I hope she hasn't found some farmers chickens and gotten shot.* I stew some more over the dangers facing a loose dog in this backwoods countryside—dangers a joyfully loose dog like Ruby can't foresee. The neighbors would be justified in shooting her if she gets into their chickens, and the local farmers won't tolerate a dog chasing their cows. *At least we haven't found her body smashed in the road.* My stomach knots up as I recall losing dogs that way before. *At least not yet.* At last, it is time for us to go to work, but Ruby has not returned. We leave messages with neighbors to watch for her, even though strangers spook her and she is unlikely to surrender herself to someone who might help. I worry about my problem girl.

Ruby is a special dog. Her antics have caused me a lot of pain and grief and have given me many reasons to spend time in prayer. So this day, too, I spend in prayer, begging for her to be spared from harm and to return safely to our fold. If she could understand the worry she is causing us, I wonder if she would be more thoughtful. Somehow, though, Siberians, like young children, don't seem to comprehend this basic fact. While they may dutifully check in, it will only be at their convenience. It could be hours or even days before they think it's necessary. I fear Ruby will be no exception.

It's different with people. My husband and I raised our children to check in with their parents from the time they are first old enough to be away on their own. We even expect our grown children to check in occasionally. We love them; care about them, and worry about them, but we also trust them to live their own lives.

With Ruby, I maintain a responsibility similar to that of the parent of a toddler. My dog may have free will, but I am still responsible for her actions and well-being. She doesn't have the comprehension or the skills to cope with the dangers of the world around her. I can't expect a small child or a dog to understand the need to check in; instead, I try to teach them the good habit.

Come evening, Bob and I head for home, worrying and praying for Ruby's safe return. We proceed up our long driveway, hoping that at any moment she will come racing out from the woods, happy to see us. But it is not so. We park at the top, and with a heavy heart, I go to the house.

Suddenly she is there. Her ears are laid back as she licks her lips and softly wags her tail. She takes a few hesitant steps towards me, uncertain if I'm going to be angry with her, but hopeful for acceptance. I slip down the side of the house, emotionally exhausted, and hold out my hand to her in reassurance. If she doesn't trust me, she still

might back away and leave again. "Ruby!" I squeak, blinking back the tears of relief. "Ruby, baby, come here. It's OK, girl. Come here." I'm slammed with forty pounds of plush fur as she leaps at me and melts into my arms for quick kisses, then bounds for the front door, eagerly squeezing in as I open it up. Ruby is home; all is right with her world.

Dear little Ruby makes me reconsider my relationship with God. He wants me to stay in His keeping. He wants to care for me and protect me. He has granted me free will, but that doesn't mean I have to run wild. In the past, I insisted on being one of the "wild and free dogs." I was proud of my independence and suffered untold miseries rather than come to the sheltering arms of the Lord. With my baptism, I surrendered to the Heavenly Master. I chose to be part of His family. Yet, how do I treat Him? I fear I have turned my back too often on the loving home He has offered. I have willfully stayed away from Him, content just to check in on Sundays—when it's convenient for me. Shouldn't I check in at other times, every day even, ensuring that I'm where I'm supposed to be and doing what He wants of me? Do I even seek to discover what His will for me is? My indifference must cause God constant pain and grief. This day I choose to live a more prayerful life. I read in my Bible, "All we, like sheep, have gone astray; we have turned everyone to his own way." Perhaps it should read, "We all, like Siberians, have gone astray, each of us has turned to our own way."

Checking In with God

Abba, Father, Daddy,
Open my eyes to Your presence.
Teach me to see You in all that is about me.
Teach me to hear You.
Teach me to listen.
Lord, teach me to share my every thought,
Hope, dream, and disappointment with You.
Teach me to talk with You as well as to walk with You.
Let me truly live each day more
Completely in Your presence.
Let me never turn my back on You
To go about my own way.

Amen.

CHAPTER FIVE

Old Coats

Ruby, being a Siberian Husky, true to form "blows coat" on a regular basis. Twice a year, from January to June and from July through December, she blossoms into her new, red fur with a creamy undercoat, and leaves behind her dingy and dry old coat. I brush her to try to control the loose hair, but for the most part, she sheds the old with little help from me.

This is not true with Keetna. My elderly dog clings to his old black coat and won't give up a hair before he has to. Come summer, when all the other dogs are sporting their shiny, new fur coats, his incoming coat is interspersed with long, dull tags of the old. I worry them out with the comb, trying to free him of the uncomfortable wool, but he shows no appreciation for my efforts. He seems to prefer the ugliness and misery with which the lingering, old coat covers him.

Eventually, I put Keetna up on the grooming table and hold him still while I pull out the old fur. The piles of shed hair collect underfoot. It's a job that takes more effort than thought, and I become introspective. Keetna reminds me of myself. I'm someone who clings to the old and familiar—the comfortable, torn coat and the well-broken-in shoes. I stubbornly cling to my old ways, my old habits, and my old self even though God has generously offered me His robe of righteousness. *How much of my "old coat" am I still clinging to? Why am I so reluctant to shed the old and put on the new?*

Sometimes a new coat comes with its obligations and burdens. For Joseph, the bright new coat of many colors triggered the jealousy of his brothers. But he accepted it anyway, knowing it pleased his father when he wore it, and he liked the way it made him feel loved.

Have I taken up the gifts my Father has given me or am I excusing myself, complaining that the burden is too hard? Recalling Joseph's new coat, I imagine him saying, "Hey, Dad, this new coat you gave me with all the colors is a real burden; it makes my brothers jealous to see all the bright yellow, blue , and red stripes. I'll just wear the blue and red stripes for now." Yet, isn't that what I do when I choose which teachings I will believe in, or when I imagine my situation is so unique that the rules don't apply? Haven't I been guilty of thinking, *'Who needs the Ten Commandments anymore? They are so dated. Today's society is capable of making their own, more relevant, rules.'* Could it be that I am simply afraid of the unknown? I prefer to cling to my old coat, my old ways—I want to hold on to the familiar, as imperfect as it is.

Keetna's old coat is history. I brush it out, and he looks and feels so much better...at least until it's time for the next change of coat. He still doesn't like the heavy grooming. He will complain when it's time to be brushed, and sometimes he will try to hide in his doghouse. Likewise, I'm still reluctant to mend my ways and put on the complete coat God offers me. I complain to God and my fellow parishioners—perhaps I always will. But I hope and pray that I can become more like Ruby and less like Keetna. *I need to accept this challenge gracefully. I need to embrace the new coat God is holding out to me—the entire coat, not just the blue and red stripes.* Keetna's grooming time becomes a time of prayer.

A Prayer to Let Go of the Old

Dear Father, please forgive me for my stubbornness,
For my determination to hang on to my old coat.
Open my eyes and my heart.
Help me to see when it is time to let go of the old and
embrace the new.
Let me accept Your brushing away of the old.
Let me trust that Your gift of a new coat is good and
desirable.
Seasons pass; times change.
What was once new and good is no longer what I need
right now.
You are all-seeing and all-caring, Lord.
You are my own generous and loving Father;
Let me accept Your grooming and Your gifts.
Beloved Father, let me see the goodness of Your gifts.
Teach me not to fear the unknown but to trust in Your
love.
Teach me to accept Your guidance, not to demand answers
on my own terms.
You have sent Your Holy Spirit.
Help me to reach out and take what He is offering.
Strengthen me so that I may willingly face my burdens.
Still the storm in my soul; calm my fears.
Stay with me throughout the journey ahead.

Amen.

CHAPTER SIX

Live for the Day

It's a sunny spring morning; the blue skies set my heart glowing. After days of gloomy rain, I can't help but feel more cheerful. It is so good to see the sun and feel its warmth as I go about my chores. I could wish every day would be this bright. Even as I think this, I know that in a few months, I will hate the blistering heat of the sun and long for the cool fall weather. Just as when winter snows were deep on the ground, I longed for the spring thaw. It would seem I'm never content.

Ruby is different. She sprawls out across the top of her doghouse, blissfully soaking up the emerging sun. All winter, she frolicked in the snow. During the spring rains, she never lost her bounce—mud puddles surely were made for dogs to splash in. Ruby lives to enjoy the moment with honest contentment. She doesn't whine and complain about current conditions like I tend to do.

I work my way through the different dog pens, scrubbing out the shiny metal water buckets and wielding the pooper-scooper. As I go about my chores, I find myself comparing my approach to life with Ruby's. I think God would prefer that I adopt Ruby's attitude. I need to savor each day for what it brings; I need to enjoy the budding leaves of spring and rejoice in the drenching rains that chase away the snow and fill the pond with water for the coming summer heat. Even when I am dreaming of snow, I still need to appreciate the warmth of summer. During the autumn, I needn't mourn the passing of the sweet flowers, especially if it means overlooking the tapestry of color the fall leaves provide.

I need to stop fussing over what might have been in the past, or what could be in the future, and enjoy what is now, in the present. I need to follow Ruby's example. She doesn't worry about what the next season will bring. With child-like innocence, she trusts that I will provide for her, but is that so bad? After all, I am her owner and guardian, and she is my fur-kid. I will take care of her.

Shouldn't I have that same child-like trust in God? He is my father and guardian, and I am His child. What does it take to convince me that He will take care of me? He has already told me to consider the lilies of the field, and Christ reminded us all that a father doesn't give a child a stone instead of bread. Why do I doubt Him so? Surely, I can just enjoy each day for what it brings and make the most of it. Days can be gloomy, and nights can be cold. Summers can bring drought, and winters can bring ice. Still, the cycles continue. Despite the problems, each season passes, and a fresh beginning presents itself once again. *Surely, I can have the faith that God will continue His care for me.*

If I truly believe in my Lord and trust Him as I say I do, I should put on a cheerful countenance and enjoy what He has given me. He has given me each day as it was meant to be. The woes of the past are just that, past. The vision of the morrow will come in due time. I can't change the weather or the day, but I can change my attitude. I can be like Ruby and enjoy it.

A Prayer for All Seasons

Lord, Creator of all things
Creator of all the earth, the sea, and the sky
Yours are the heavens in all their glory.
Yours is the sunrise; Yours is the sunset
Yours is the moon; Yours are the stars.

You give us the sunshine to warm the earth each spring
You give us the rain to water the emerging greens.
You give us the wild winds of March
And the gentle breezes of June.
You give us summers accented by a passion of
bright flowers.
You give us the crisp autumn that turns the summer
leaves into a riot of color.
And in the winter, You blanket all with the sparkling snow.
You give us each season, in its turn.
For this, I thank You, Lord.
Open my eyes to the glory You have placed before me.
Help me to enjoy the beauty of each season as it comes
And, in the darkest winter,
to trust that spring will come again.

Amen.

CHAPTER SEVEN

What Are You Good For?

It's time to take the dogs for a training run. I sort through the harnesses, trying to decide who I will hook up for today's workout. I choose the purple harness for Abbie, and Corrie's green one—they will be my leads. *I like Flash in wheel, he's a good strong dog,* I think, gathering up his blue one. I haven't taken Darby out recently, so I'll put him in wheel along with Flash. The black harness completes my selection for this first run. On my second run, I'll take Storm and Breeze as leads, and Beth can do wheel with her mother,

Gale. That leaves Ruby, Kodi, and Keetna for another day. The soft nylon web harnesses don't make any sound to me as I take them in hand, but the dogs instantly know it's time. I walk out to the kennel; the dogs start their excited howls competing for my attention "Me! Me! Take me! It's my turn! Choose me!"

"Not today, Ruby. You wait. This time I need Corrie and Flash." She gives me her soulful look, sadly agreeing to wait but believing next time she'll get to come. Guilt nags me as to why I don't take her more often, but still I leave her behind.

Ruby is good for nothing—and good for everything. She doesn't shine as a lead dog; she is possibly the slowest of my dogs, and certainly isn't any powerhouse for pulling like a good wheel dog. Most often, she is the one left behind in reserve because I believe another dog will do the job better. Yet I know I can put Ruby anywhere on the team. She may be a lightweight, but she works hard, regardless if she is in front of the team or working in the wheel position. She puts all her energy into the job at hand, no matter how tired she is, or how late it is, or how many loops of the trail she has already run. She focuses on pulling, on getting the job done, not on who is in harness beside her, or if her teammates are doing their share. This cheerful, hardworking attitude makes her a valuable sled dog. So why don't I use her all the time instead of just as a substitute? Perhaps the failing is in me, not her. *Perhaps I should be making an effort to see her good points instead of degrading her for what she isn't.*

What about the way I look at others? *Do I bypass the hardworking ordinary women in favor of the divas? Do I prefer temperamental celebrities to honest workers?* Sure, it's nice to work with the brightest and best. Who doesn't want to surround themselves with great people? But there is great value in the average person; I just need to see them. Perhaps I need to build my human team with fewer stars and more workers. I have to admit that I fail miserably in this area. I don't want to be associated with anything less than stellar quality.

The question that naturally follows is harder to face. *Do I accept myself, with all my weaknesses, faults, and imperfections? Do I love myself?* Jesus tells us in the Great Commandment to "Love one another as you love yourself." If I don't love myself, if I have no self-respect, how can I love others the way Jesus has asked?

But I do respect myself, don't I? Yes, the same way I respect Ruby. But I don't value myself any more than I value her over others; I am guilty of selling us both short. Just as I wonder why I have failed to consider Ruby's worth, I also wonder why I have failed to give myself credit. Could it be that I have confused self-respect with self-awareness and self-esteem? Self-awareness is recognition of one's personal identity, an understanding of who I am, what my gifts, strengths, limitations, and weaknesses are. Self-esteem focuses placing value on who I am, the way that I am. I don't need a mirror to see my shortcomings in that aspect. I can see it all when I think of Ruby. I look at myself and see the weaknesses, the failures, just as I see what Ruby can't do so well. I don't see my strengths or my gifts. The way I love myself is important—if I have no self-esteem, how can I love myself? I can't have real self-respect if I believe I am good for nothing any more than I can give Ruby, or anyone else, my full respect if I don't see their value. I need to see my worth as one of God's own before I can see others as God's children and appreciate them equally.

I don't suppose Ruby reflects on her value to the sled team or struggles with self-esteem as I do. Still, that's no excuse for me to ignore the status of myself and others as children of God. I know God loves me. He has allowed me to be part of His family—he has adopted me as His own, despite my many shortcomings. He accepts me as I am, just as I accept Ruby with all her shortcomings and as she accepts me with all my faults. I need to make an effort to discover my own God-given gifts and put them to use the way He has intended. Only then can I learn to accept others who don't meet my ideal of perfection.

Each Sunday in church, I pray, "Forgive us our trespasses as we forgive those who trespass against us." Perhaps I should pray, "Forgive me my weaknesses, my faults, my imperfections, as I forgive the shortcomings and failings of others."

Just As I Am

Lord, You love me as I am.
You loved me when I was young and capable,
You love me still when I am old and stiff.
You loved me when I was slender,
You love me still now that I am overweight.
Lord, Yours is a model of love for me to follow.
Help me to love others equally no matter what
shape they are in.
Teach me to be accepting, not judgmental.
It doesn't matter to You if a person is intelligent
or slow to learn.
Help me to develop the same ability to accept others.
Dear Lord, people of all sizes, shapes,
and abilities are equally precious to You.
Let them all be precious to me, also.

Amen.

CHAPTER EIGHT

Shut Up and Listen

Race day has arrived. We pull into the parking area with the dog truck, unload the dogs and snap them to their drop lines to stretch and relieve themselves. I offer each a drink of water, and then head to the driver's meeting to get the last-minute details for the day's event. From the dog area comes a riot of sound as the dogs voice their excitement. It's difficult to hear the instructions over the cacophony. I try to tune out the noise and focus on the race marshal's directions.

My race isn't until 10 a.m. so I have plenty of time to grab a donut and chat with friends before heading back to the truck. I give each dog a few moments of hugs and scritches before digging out the harnesses and lines. The sled is already unloaded and snubbed to the truck in preparation for hook-up. I tie my number bib in place and get out the tack box. I just have to put the harnesses on and get the dogs lined out, then we'll be ready.

"Settle down, Ruby!" She dances and squirms as I try to get her bright green harness on and she "woos" loudly as I move her to the line. "Ruby! Easy! You're going to trip me!" Her front feet paw the air as I lift her by her collar to bounce on her hind legs. It's the safest way to keep control over her as she lives up to her nickname "The Ditzy Blonde." By the time I hook up the other dogs, I'm panting myself. I go back to Ruby and fasten her tug. I save that for last because her impatient circling while she waits will twist the line into a snarl if I snap it up too early.

At last, everyone is hooked up and ready. My helper leads the dogs to the starting area as the eager dogs add their voices to the rising din and the butterflies in my stomach take wing. Once we are in the starting chute, Ruby and her teammates throw themselves against the harnesses in an effort to break free from restraint. I call out "Hike" as the hands of the chute aids holding them in fall away and the dogs, suddenly silent, lunge forward down the trail.

"Good dogs," I call to them. "Good girl Ruby, good girl Abbey. Let's go." A snow-laden pine empties its icy burden down my back. "Argh! That's cold!" I shriek. The dogs ahead of me twitch their ears, wondering if I'm talking to them. "It's OK. You're doing fine. Ahead, girls. Pick it up, now! We need to be a little faster. That's good, Ruby. Good girl, Beth…" I continue my barrage aimed at the canine ears for another quarter of a mile until the first turn off in the trail. "Gee!" I call, "Corrie! Abbey! Gee!" My leaders ignore me as they plunge on straight. "No! Whoa, girls, whoa!" I stomp on the brake and the sled jerks to a stop. Abbey turns back to look at me as if asking what the problem is. "Gee," I insist, "Gee." Corrie and Abbey swing to the right, and I release the brake. We plunge down the correct trail and I start up my chatter again, but this time to God.

Oh God, Please let me do well during this race. I don't want to be last. Can you make sure the dogs all do well, too? I need Abbey and Corrie to make the turns today. Please don't let me mess up."

As we swish down the snow-covered trail, I reflect, *'Silence is golden.' When I don't shut up, the dogs tune me out just as I turned a deaf ear to their unintelligible noise this morning. Does God tune me out, too? Probably not, but if I don't quiet myself,*

how can I hear His response?

Prayer isn't meant to be a monologue. My prayer should be part of a conversation, a give-and-take scenario. When I pray, I wish I could trust that God hears my prayers. It's so easy to believe He isn't listening to me when I don't get the desired answer. How many times is the reality simply that I don't hear God speaking to me, or that I pretend I don't hear what He is telling me because I don't like what He is saying? Rather like Ruby, with her selective Siberian hearing. She acts like she doesn't hear me call her, but the truth is, she doesn't want to come in yet, so she will continue her exploring or playing until I become persistent and demanding. Then she will give me a surprised look as if she had no idea I had been calling to her.

I suspect that all too often I am like Ruby, selectively hearing only what I want to hear, only when I want to hear it. *Do I hear my neighbor's distress, or is it too inconvenient for me? I've been raised on independence. Do I value it so much that I can't respect another's need for help? Or is it my own attitude of not needing anyone that deafens me to their pleas? Do I mentally condemn the poor and down-trodden, convinced they somehow aren't worthy of being heard?*

Ruby tunes me out because of the distractions around her—the chittering squirrel, the earthy smells, the flash of a passing chickadee, or the romping of the other dogs in their play yard. I tune my Father God out when I let the noise of daily life be a higher priority than my connection to Him, or when I'm so busy talking to him in prayer that I don't just shut up and listen. There is nothing to say I'll like his response, or that his answer won't still be, "No," but if I open the channel both ways, I can experience real communication, real prayer.

Shh. Be Quiet

Lord, teach me silence.
Open my ears to Your Holy Word.
Let me recognize Your beloved Spirit
In the quiet solitude as He reaches out to me.
Help me to discard my selective hearing.
Shh. Be quiet.
Turn off the music, turn down the lights.
The day isn't over but the time for prayer is here.
Shh. Be quiet.
It's God's turn to speak.

CHAPTER NINE

Bread That Is Broken

It's bath time for Ruby. I've placed her special shampoo alongside the tub, and a stack of clean towels sits on the bathroom floor in easy reach. I'm wearing an old swimsuit since I will undoubtedly end up nearly as wet as her. The grooming table is set up in the living room with the dryer and all the brushes and combs I expect to need. With everything ready for the challenge, I put Ruby on her leash and drag her to the tub as her body goes rigid in protest.

"Sorry, girl. I know you hate bath time, but you need to look pretty for tomorrow." She whines back at me and struggles again to jump out of the tub. "Nope. You have to stay," I insist. "Let's get you soaped up." I spread the doggie shampoo across her back and down her chest and begin scrubbing. In the morning Ruby will be going with me to a local elementary school for a demonstration on dog sledding. Normally I don't bathe the dogs for such an occasion, but Ruby has been playing in the mud and has become grubby.

After a thorough rinse, Ruby drowns me with a couple of good shakes, and I move her to the grooming table in the next room. I turn the blow dryer on high and let the rest of the water spray off her along with a cloud of wet hair she has suddenly decided to shed. Eventually, she is dry enough that I can begin the brushing to fluff out her coat.

Ruby will never have the super-fluffy coat typical of a show dog. It's harsh and tight, good for keeping warm and for shedding snow and ice. It's the coat of a working dog, and there is no shame in that. I love the way Ruby looks even if some show people might look at her with disdain. They too often limit themselves into just seeing the outer beauty and ignoring the inside of the dog.

I love all my dogs. It's not just the way they look, or how they perform on the team. Each one is an individual, a distinct personality. Storm is a firecracker, bursting with energy. Corrie is playful, finding a game in anything. Breeze is a gentle softy, except when it's time to run, then she's all drive. Xander is my peacemaker. He's quick to shove his way in between two grumbling dogs, stopping a fight before it begins. And of course, there is Ruby—bouncing around, never still, eager to shower love and kisses on any friend, new or old. I value each individual dog and appreciate their uniqueness. They don't need to do anything to earn my love. Their everyday behavior may give me pleasure or distress, but it doesn't change my love for them.

God loves me the same way, my heart whispers to me. I am loved just as I am. I can choose by my actions to please Him or bring Him pain. My problem with that is trying to discern what pleases Him. No, it's more than that. It's also a matter of putting aside my wants in order to do what He wishes. There is also the question of understanding that

God's will may seem restrictive or unfair, but I still need to trust His way is best.

Does Ruby understand my role in caring for her? Just now, at bath time, probably not. For sure, she isn't appreciative, I think as she struggles to jump down from the table for the fifth time in ten minutes. *Does she even care about what I go through as long as she gets what she wants? Is that the way I treat God? Do I struggle in protest and seek to do my will, rather than His?*

Ruby is a working dog, not a contestant in a beauty pageant. Her value is transformed by purpose. It makes sense to believe that my value is also transformed by purpose. She was born to run in the snow; her life's work is pulling a sled. *What about me? Is my value transformed by purpose? Do I even know my purpose?* The words of Christ penetrate my thoughts. "This is my body, given up for you." Bread, broken and shared—the body of Christ was broken on the cross so that we might have everlasting life. *How has my life been shared? Have I allowed it to be broken for others? What does that mean, anyway?* I look at Ruby's coat again. Living her life the way it was intended costs her something. Her thick coat may keep her warm, but the wear of the harness marks it. Even now, I can see the light bands marking her fur where the harness has rubbed the darker tips off her hair.

When Ruby works in harness, she is giving of herself for the team, for the common good. God understands this. To be of the most value to us, He had to take on human form and live an ordinary life. Because he did this, I have no doubt God understands the problems I encounter in my life every day. God, the Son, could have been just a model of perfection, but He chose to be more. By engaging Himself in my daily living, He engages me in a heavenly relationship with the Father. Through Christ, God became a tangible part of my life today. I wonder if I really understand the awesomeness of this gift.

What about me? Am I fully engaged in a relationship with the Father? Am I willing to make sacrifices for the good of all? What is my real purpose in life? I carry those questions with me to bed at night.

The next day the sled and the dogs are loaded up in the truck. A gaggle of fourth and fifth-graders soon get the chance to meet the sled dogs and learn about teamwork. When we finish our sledding demonstration, Ruby gives me a happy grin and slobbery kisses. I share her joy with a job well done, but my body aches, I'm tired, and my throat is sore from all the talking. But the job isn't really over—I still have to load the dogs and equipment back up, drive home, unload, and put everything away. Naturally, Ruby thinks I should be free to play with her a little longer. Ruby, I don't believe that you understand the totality of effort involved in what you seem to think is just a day of play. In fact, you probably don't understand my relationship with you and the rest of the kennel any more than I fully understand my relationship with God. Yet that didn't stop Him from sharing his life with me—and with a world of others, too.

Ruby's purpose involves giving herself for the good

of the team. Christ also gave himself for the good of all. *What about me? Have I discovered my purpose yet? What part of the team of humanity does God intend for me to work at?* It seems like the goals I've strived for involve concepts like making a lot of money, being popular, having the respect of others, being recognized as brighter, stronger, or more talented. *What about the concept of emptying myself, of giving others the same love and respect that I would like to have?*

Christ is the Bread of Life that is broken and shared with others. Could that mean in order to be Christ-like I need to break myself open, discover who I am, and share my life with others? *Perhaps. Then again, once I am broken open and can see who I am, maybe I can begin to understand others.* Suddenly, I realize that this is the core of Christian compassion. Instead of insulating myself, I need be open and vulnerable so I can fully understand and love others.

There can be no doubt that Christ gave everything for mankind, yet at the moment, I cannot name much that I have given, except where it benefits me. That is a dismaying thought. I need to not see others as obstacles to getting what I want out of life, but rather seek to understand them better, so that we may become partners in purpose.

An Understanding Heart

I may never understand the whys and wherefores
of this life.
I may never understand how evil can be so rampant
Or why war and violence seem to be the norm.
But Lord, could You please help me to understand
my neighbor?
To understand other individuals on a personal level,
To relate to their joys and their sorrows,
To comprehend their motivations and their satisfactions,
This, O Lord, is an understanding heart.
This, O Lord, would enrich my relationship
with my neighbors
So that I may better help them.
If you would give me a gift, dear Father,
Bless me with an understanding heart.

Amen.

CHAPTER TEN

False Images

Ruby has no clothes. Well, she does in that she has a collar, and she has a functional harness, but she doesn't wear clothes to change her appearance, to attract others, to create an artificial image, or to advertise her prestige. She doesn't wear jewelry or make-up, either. We, as a society, don't find this a problem. After all, Ruby is a sled dog, not a status symbol.

Sometimes I see a young woman parading down the street, and I think, If only she could see herself in a mirror, and if only the image reflected showed what she really looked like. While perhaps the mask she has put on displays her actual self, more likely she would be embarrassed. Or would the problem be that she thinks she would be more embarrassed if her friends could see who she is on the inside?

What about me? Can I say I don't dress to create an artificial image? I am constantly bombarded with expectations to dress to allure men; I am encouraged to advertise my sexuality, to demonstrate my worth with costly jewelry, to dye my hair and paint my face to camouflage my natural looks. Perhaps it is a sign of innate insecurity that I am tempted to listen and reach for externals to recreate myself.

So far, I have resisted the admonitions to color my hair or conceal my wrinkles, but when I look in the mirror at night, I am dissatisfied with the image I see. I am cross with myself for what I look like. The question is, whose image should I be driven trying to imitate—the latest rock star, the current celebrity, Vogue's concept of beauty? Whatever happened to being created in God's image? By conforming to society's expectations of dress and beauty, am I dressing myself in falsehoods like the emperor in his new clothes? Have I shut my eyes to the reality of who I am? Is my deeply-rooted insecurity letting me parade around decorated as something I'm not, pretending I'm not vulnerable, pretending that others can't see through the façade to whom I really am?

I try to convince myself that it is part and parcel of conforming to the expectations of society. I would claim it's a matter of dignity that I have certain appearances to keep up to preserve the respect of Christians. When I dig deeper into my heart, I think that by wrapping myself in empty pride, I fall into the trap of believing I am more entitled to respect than another person is.

Ruby, on the other hand, has no dignity. She happily throws herself at anyone, begging for pets, or for a treat. She rolls over and exposes her tummy for extra scritches, ready to reward the giver with her sloppy doggie kisses. Is it possible that my vision of dignity is nothing more than a false sense of pride? What can I possibly claim as worthy of my pride? Isn't all I have, all I am, a gift from God?

The dogs in my kennel are a lot smarter: Ruby, for one, doesn't care about the externals. She is herself and doesn't make excuses. She wears her God-given fur coat without seeming regret for what color it is. She sees clearly out of her amber eyes without caring that many expect a "real Siberian" to have blue eyes. *Lord, help me to be more like Ruby. Help me to cast aside foolish pride. Open my eyes so that I can tell the difference between popular glamor and real beauty, between false dignity and the garment of your righteousness. Help me to re-create myself in Your image. Help me to recognize just what that image is.*

Show Me

Lord, hear my prayers.
Bless me with Your grace.
Show me the way.

Open my mind
That I may understand
Who I am and what I can do.
Show me who I am.

Open my eyes
That I may see Your glory,
And in it, the goal You have set before me.
Show me where You would have me go.

Open my ears
That I may hear the cries of Your people,
Even when they have no voice.
Show me how I may help.

Open my heart
That I may long to do Your will
And become Your true servant.
Show me Your way.

Amen.

CHAPTER ELEVEN

Death and Dignity

When I arrive home from work at the studio, it is immediately obvious there is a major problem. While all the dogs are bouncing and eager for me to let them out, someone had left a deposit on the kitchen floor, a black, tarry, bloody stool. I don't know who did it, but from the appearance, she doesn't have long in this world. With three seniors and a foolish counter surfer, it could have been any of the housedogs. Within an hour, there is little question. Sitka, Ruby's great-grandmother, is fading fast. By bedtime, she can barely stand and can only walk a few steps at a time. She doesn't seem to be in any pain, but the look in her eyes says she is ready to go. Earlier, we had decided she would get only palliative care, aiming for her comfort, not to prolong her dying. It is hard to say goodnight, knowing she probably won't be with us in the morning.

When I came downstairs in the morning to let everyone out, Sitka isn't at the door with the others. I find her sprawled in her crate, at peace with the world. Sitting down next to her, I reach out to give her cold, stiff body a pat. She jerks awake and sits up with a start, indignant that I would sneak up on her and poke her like that. I rock backwards, not sure who is more startled, Sitka or me. After she eats some breakfast, she goes out and takes care of her business—more bloody stools.

Sitka has looked across the bridge at death and changed her mind, but her health still holds her at the brink. She is reluctant to make that final crossing, even though it is obvious to others that her time has arrived. She is fourteen and a half years old, has cancer, and cannot tolerate any anesthetic. Several times now, the vet has given her only a short time to live.

The old girl selects the middle of the kitchen as her spot to rest. It's awkward for us, but we'll manage. Besides, she has no bladder or bowel control left, and it's the easiest place to clean. I wonder if I ought to take her to the vet and have her put down, but I currently have a personal hang-up with playing God. Sitka is still struggling to live, so it smacks of being more an issue of my convenience. I've had to end the lives of past animals, and still suffer from pain and guilt. We decide to let her live as long as she chooses since she doesn't seem to be in pain.

The next evening that decision is strained to the max as Sitka has repeated convulsions. We expected each breath to be her last. Come morning, however, she is relaxed and raised her head to take a good drink of water. She can't stand but is able to shift around and change positions. I spend quite a bit of time brushing her and cleaning her up.

Sitka's status reminds me so much of my mother's last days that, at times, I can barely stand it. It seems that with each death, I find my feelings of family and pets more and more intertwined. I sit beside Sitka and pray to my God. *Are You their God, too? Do my dogs love and serve You? Do they have their own religion and forms of worship?* Who am I to say? They are God's creatures, I know, but if there is more to it, how can they pass on their history, culture, and religion? We pull pups away from their canine families at a shockingly tender age. I shake my head wishing I had someone to talk with about it. My neighbors wouldn't understand; they would just say, "They are just dogs. Get a life, woman!"

It's Monday again, and when I return home, Sitka is sprawled out, once again looking more dead than alive. Even though she is nearly deaf and misses a lot, she must sense me coming because she suddenly sits up and looks at me, she even stands for a moment, and I swear she wags her tail a stroke or two. This is wild because she never greeted me like that when she was well. Definitely, our relationship is changing.

Someone suggests that Sitka is not ready to leave because she still has a job here on Earth. I think that is just the case—I've learned so much from her this past week about life and death. We struggle to preserve dignity, and for that reason, we encourage euthanasia for our pets. But where is dignity? Is it in the circumstances surrounding a person? Do elderly people who have lost bladder control no longer have dignity? Would it be fitting to determine an accident has stripped a quadriplegic of dignity and that he would be better off dead?

Perhaps dignity is found in the way one acts, but wouldn't that mean a sleeping or unconscious person no longer has dignity? My dog doesn't act like my father, yet, I would say both have dignity. What actions make a person or a dog no longer demonstrate dignity? Does one such action strip them forever? My mother, on her deathbed, held a great deal of dignity to me. But did she show it to the nurses who didn't know her as I did? Perhaps dignity is in the eyes of the beholder. If this is true, then is dying with dignity more about when the caretaker is ready to let the patient go, not when the patient is ready to die?

It may be inappropriate to equate our fur-kids with humans, but I'm finding that while dealing with Sitka, I am reliving my mother's last days as well as looking at the grim future of terminal cancer my dad is facing. I'm finding issues coming out that I apparently buried rather than resolved. I'm grateful to Sitka for helping me this way. I guess there is a purpose to her lingering.

On a more disturbing note, as this ordeal proceeds, I'm finding myself thinking less like an animal welfare supporter and more like an animal rights extremist. That scares the heck out of me. Sometimes it isn't comforting or convenient to think of dogs the same as I do people. The very thought challenges too many of my customs and values.

Dying with dignity—it's something I seek to achieve, but how can I make it happen unless it's clear in my mind what this intangible dignity consists of? I probe my innermost thoughts, trying to find an answer I can live with.

Dignity can't be about how quickly or painlessly one dies. It has to be more about how one chooses to live the life they do have. That may be it. In the end, it could be about choices. Dignity involves not what one is able to do, whether or not the dogs or terminally ill people can care for themselves, but the choices they are able to make and how the choices are honored.

Sitka collapsed twice before in her life and hovered near death for days, unwilling to let go. Each time, I coaxed her body back to health and (hopefully) happiness. This last time I know there will be no recovery, but it is hard to determine how much care she should have. Dignity isn't just in the eyes of the caretaker—it can be created or destroyed by the caretaker. When Sitka doesn't eat because she is too weak, I gently spoon food into her. The last day, she is able to eat, but pushes aside her dish and rejects all food. Initially, force-feeding was assistance and did not belittle her, but to do so now will strip her of any remaining dignity. It is her choice, one of the few left to her.

Choices: it may well be the difference between slavery and servitude. Animal rights extremists claim companion animals are slaves, but if they have the opportunity to make choices, doesn't that change it all? As with parents and small children, we must take charge and make some choices for our pets. Surely, there are plenty left to them, if we recognize them and honor their choices.

Sitka made the choice to fight for her life. She is ready to cross the bridge and is doing her best to live her life right up to the last hours. But I have to make choices, too. Her deteriorating condition requires more time than I have available, or perhaps it is more time than I am willing to allow on a prioritized list of daily needs (like going to work, eating, and sleeping). I have to choose if I am to ignore her and let her literally rot in place, if I should do what I can even if it means letting her die more slowly, or if I should choose euthanasia and release us both.

Euthanasia presents itself as the destruction of hope; for people, it's either murder or it's suicide. Either way, I see it as a refusal to accept that we have a soul and that there is an afterlife. I cannot accept that for human lives, but it is different with animals. God has charged me to be a good steward. He calls me to care for my animals from the beginning of life through death. The choice of life, of dignity, therefore belongs not just to Sitka but also to me. It may be my choice, but I find that I don't want to be God. I only pray that He will guide me through this difficult time.

Be My Guide

Be my guide, dear Lord,
In everything I say.
Help me to be quiet when I shouldn't speak
And to speak up with confidence when the time is right.
Give me the right words to say and help me to recognize
the right times to say them.

Be my guide, dear Lord,
In everything I do.
Help me to keep my hands off when I shouldn't interfere
And direct my actions when it is the correct time
to step in and assist.
Give me the wisdom to see when different actions
are needed.

Be my guide, dear Lord,
In everything I think.
Keep me from being judgmental.
And direct my mind to see You in others.
Keep my thoughts from being lost in the darkness.

You, O Lord, are my light.
Your love, quiet but firm, steadies me through life.
You, O Lord, are my role model.
Let me not stray, but guide me always in Your way.

Amen.

CHAPTER TWELVE

Putting Away Christmas

The Christmas season is ending, and it's time to put away the decorations and lights that have brightened the holidays. Carefully, I remove each fragile ornament and tuck it into its place in the box. The dogs gather around to watch what I'm doing. Ruby has left off playing outside and is now underfoot. She sniffs at the delicate glass ornament in my hand. It's one of my favorites, with a classic nativity scene painted on gold glass. She cocks her head and studies me with curiosity, trying to figure out what I'm doing. Perhaps she is only wondering if I will drop something interesting to chew on, but as I look into her amber eyes, I can imagine her, like a precocious toddler, asking a deeper question.

What are you doing, Mommy? I'm putting away Christmas. *Why?* Christmas is over. *Has it gone away?* Well, not gone, just that it's time to pack it all up out of sight. *Why?*

Why indeed? I can say that the time for holiday cheerfulness, for special activities, has passed. I can say that the time for showing our outward displays of faith is over, that those who persist in leaving up their decorations, their manifestations of their Christian faith, are ridiculed. I can say that it is not proper to leave such things out for others to see after the pre-set time frame. At least that is what the popular culture would have me believe.

Suddenly, I stop and ask myself, Could that be what others think about my Christian faith, that it's just a cosmetic display? Am I projecting to others the reality I claim to be true? My profession of faith needs to run a lot deeper than just an outward display.

This year, as in years past, I hung Christmas lights on the top of the kennel panels to illuminate the dog yard. The dogs don't need these blatant decorations to declare a joyful season. With smiles on their faces, they maintain an attitude of "holiday cheer" all year long; however, during the winter, I need lights to see by in order to feed and water the dogs after dark. Perhaps it is similar to using Christ to light my way in the darkness of the unknown. Just as the Christmas season lights the heart of the dark winter, I can claim His newly-come light into the world to guide me through my own darkness. *Why should I put that away? Don't I need his guidance all year around?*

During the Christmas season, it is excusable to show our religion to the world. Manifestations of Christian love and generosity are popular news items; however, once January rolls around, it's on to something else. *When the New Year is rung in, am I expected to tuck my faith away along with the rest of the Christmas decorations?* It sometimes seems so. Outside of the Christmas season, it is not proper to let others see the visible signs of Christian faith unless it is during church. Others may feel that if I pray in public, make the sign of the cross, or shout, "Praise be!" and "Amen!" that I am imposing my beliefs on them. In this secular culture where we strive to be all-accepting and politically correct, faith has become a personal matter. As such, displaying Christian symbols and public demonstrations of faith are no longer encouraged.

Some people declare that Christmas is for children, and it has a different place in the lives of adults. But we are called to come like children to the Lord, with open and trusting hearts. It is a basic tenet of my faith that God's own son, Jesus, was born of Mary in Bethlehem. I am reminded each Christmas to accept Him, to welcome Him into my life. But once the season is over what happens next? Do I put the Christ Child away after Christmas like one of the ornaments? Shall I box him up like the fragile ornament I'm holding in my hand? Do I set Him aside like a winter coat hung in the closet until it gets cold again, or until I have more time, or until I need Him again? Maybe I'm guilty of keeping Him on display, perpetually an infant, like Christmas lights left out all year. I think I need to take that newborn infant and nurture Him, allowing Him to grow to fullness. Would anyone notice if I did? Shouldn't it be obvious? Uncomfortably, I think, yes, it should be.

Regardless of what may be politically correct, my faith should not be so private that it is non-existent to others. I shouldn't "light a lamp and put it under a bushel." But neither should I be like the scribes of Christ's time, making my faith a matter of superficial public display, like a tawdry Christmas spectacle put out by someone who isn't even nominally Christian.

Maybe the "decorations" I am concerned about putting away should be the ones expressed by my soul to the public. I should take a lesson from Ruby. I can keep that cheerful feeling out front; I can hang out a smile and a generous attitude all year long. That string of gaudy lights and a tinseled tree at Christmas are, after all, just symbols of a commercialized holiday. The real symbols of my faith should not be put away. They should be displayed by my soul, year round, for all to see. Ruby wags her tail and "woofs" gently in agreement.

Tenderly, I pick up Baby Jesus from the crèche and place him in the box to be stored away with the other figures until next year. It's dark now. Although I have put away the decorations, I am determined to keep Christmas in my heart all year through. As I head out to the dog yard to do the evening chores, I smile at the strings of multicolored lights hanging from the tops of the kennel panels. They can stay up, a reminder to me from Ruby and her companions, that the peace and joy of Christmas can light my way throughout my life.

A Prayer to Nourish Christmas

Lord, dearest Father,
You gave us Your son, a newborn Babe.
You gave us the Prince of Peace.
You gave us hope for a new tomorrow.
Lord, just as a newborn cannot thrive without nurturing,
Peace and Hope cannot thrive without our support.
Teach me, o Lord, to care for this tender flower of peace.
Teach me to feed this newborn hope.
Teach me to grow this new tomorrow
Every day, every week, every month, all year round
Teach me to hold the promise of Christmas in my heart
Let me nourish the Christ Child
And cause Him to grow in me.
Let me not set aside Your great gift
But proudly emblazon it across my heart
Displaying Your love for all to see.

Amen.

CHAPTER THIRTEEN

Love and Don't Look Back

"Five, four, three, two, one! Go musher!" The team plunges forward, and we're off down the trail. It's me and the dogs, working as a team. Ruby and the others focus on the trail and the race. She may not like to run as much as some of my other dogs, but she doesn't forget the job at hand. Birds singing in the woods and flitting squirrels don't distract her. She never slacks on her assignment.

God has given me an assignment. My job is to love, not just family members or people who are nice to me, but everyone, even my enemies. It's hard for me to be as focused on that job as Ruby is on hers. I get caught up in the flow of life, my job, my daily chores, and the requirements of daily living. My own squirrels—politics, disagreeable people, and my self-centered desires—distract me all too often.

The team bounds out of the woods and onto a wide stretch of the trail. Ahead of me, another team has pulled to the side while the musher hurries to straighten out a tangle. "On by!" I call to my team. If my dogs stop to visit, we will just make the tangle worse, and both teams will suffer. I whistle to my dogs, encouraging them to stay focused on the trail at hand. We charge on ahead as the trail turns back into the trees.

From behind, I can hear another musher calling to his team. I worry that he is going to catch and pass me, and I look back over my shoulder. That, of course, is the moment the runners hit an unexpected ridge of ice; the sled bucks in protest, and I lose my balance. Struggling to remain upright, I am no longer focused and in charge of the sled, but reduced to clinging desperately to the handlebars as it careens down the trail. Unheeding of my peril, the dogs continue around the corner, dragging the now tipped-over sled, with me bouncing behind hanging on with one hand and a prayer. A spray of icy snow crystals stings my face. *How long can I hang on this way?* "Whoa! Whoa, dogs. Whoa!"

Too often, this is the story of my life. I worry about the competition, about comparing myself with others, and I lose track of the path ahead. God wants me to be myself. He doesn't compare me to others; He just wants me to finish the race. Likewise, Ruby doesn't care if we come in first or last.

God, I made such horrible mistakes last time. When I think about what I've done, I'm so embarrassed. Stop. I remind myself once again; that is in the past, behind me. You forgave me, Lord. Why can't I stop beating myself up for what has already happened? Why can't I forgive myself? My self-punishing tirade continues despite myself. What if I goof up again? I probably will, You know. How can You keep forgiving me for the same things, over and over again?

The dogs come to a reluctant stop. I right the sled and climb back on the runners as they bang against the harnesses, eager to be off and running again.

"OK, hike!" The sled jerks forward, nearly upsetting me again, but this time I'm prepared. With a quick look down, I check to make sure the snow hook is secured and won't bounce loose. As the team rushes forward, I nearly miss the sign marking the split in the trail, but a last minute "gee" to the dogs gets us headed in the right direction.

I need to stop looking over my shoulder. Reliving the past isn't doing anyone any good. I need to really believe that God has forgiven me. It's time to forgive myself and face forward, to the future. The trail ahead may have more surprises, but if I take and live each moment as it comes, I'll manage. It should be enough that I'm doing as God asks. I must learn to make it enough; focusing on the trail He has lovingly laid out for me is the only way to be true to God's calling.

The dogs are running smoothly now as the trail comes out of the woods again. The bright sun bounces across the snow, shattering into a million sparkles. Chickadees call from the pines beside us, the only sound other than the hissing of the runners through the soft snow. With my eyes on the trail ahead of me, I'm filled with a sense of oneness with God's creation.

On the Trail

Lord, it's me.
I'm here, wanting You, needing You.
There is an ache in my heart, a longing to walk with You.
I think to walk with You must be the most precious thing
I could hope for.
But I can't do it if I'm looking over my shoulder.
I need to focus on You, keeping my eyes
on where I'm going.
Our relationship isn't based on a comparison with others.
Your Way is not posted with direction signs
made by other's progress.
Our relationship is personal–
You and me.
Help me O Lord. Help me put on the blinders.
Blind me to the desire to compare myself to others.
Blind me to the worldly distractions.
Keep my eyes on the path ahead.
Keep me focused on The Way
Be my guide.

Amen.

CHAPTER FOURTEEN

Feed My Sheep

It's kennel feeding time again. The dogs, as usual, clamor for their supper. They bounce around, on top of the doghouses and down again, nearly knocking me over as they jump on me to show their enthusiasm. Ruby seems convinced that barking loudly in my ear will hurry me along. I guess God's plan for me is not to "Feed my sheep," but to "Feed the dogs."

"Feed my sheep." Historically, Christ gives the command to Peter, but I believe that He also has given it to each one of us. As a practicing Christian, I have to believe Christ is speaking those words to me.

Confused, as usual, by the seemingly unrealistic demands, I throw it back to Him and ask for clarification. Lord, with what shall I feed them? Look at me—I have nothing. I am nothing! Lord, how can I even begin to care for your people? No, You'll have to ask someone else. Either that or bless me with a lottery win, so I have the wherewithal to give to others.

If I were wealthy, I could donate generous amounts

of money to worthy causes. I wouldn't be restricted by having to sort through which was more important. I would be free to decide for myself which causes I wanted to support. Of course, I would still have plenty for my family, my hobbies, and the things I want. I wouldn't even have to go to work every day. I would be free to do the things I wanted to, to participate in the activities I wanted to. I could spend a day with Habitat for Humanity or a week with Haitian Relief, if I chose. Yes, with enough money, I would be in control. I could indeed feed Your sheep.

I, I, I. O Lord, where would You, be in my life if I were wealthy? Would I be so wrapped in my own interests and in filling my needs that I would lose track of You? Would I be the rich man struggling to get the camel through the needle's eye instead of the widow giving her mite? I would fear for my very soul if I were to become so wealthy. Surely, I would be one who gave from my excess, rather than from my own self. Somehow, Father, I don't think that's what You intend. I don't think that's what it means to be a devout Christian.

Ruby gives of herself. When I hook her up to the sled, she puts her entire heart into the work at hand. She is a wonderful dog to have available when we are doing sled rides for kids. Leaning into the harness, she gives her all. When other dogs are ready to quit, bored with the endless loops, I can count on her to keep going, ready to pull just one more youngster around for an unforgettable ride. When we visit the schools, classes after classes of children mob the dogs; she is always ready for one more child, ready to accept their tentative pats or their overenthusiastic hugs. Ruby has no money, no excess to give from. Ruby has only herself to offer. Yes, Ruby answers the call of "Feed my sheep," in her own doggie way. Can I offer any less to my Lord's children, His sheep? Maybe it doesn't take money to feed others. Maybe there are other ways to nourish His flock.

I guess, Lord, that if I am to do Your work, to feed your sheep, I'll have to do it as a poor person unless there is a lottery win in my future. But to give of my very self—how can I? Lord, I am nothing. Was it Moses who insisted he couldn't manage by himself? You, Lord, reminded him that he had Aaron to help. Dear Father, You have given me Ruby. Is she to be my helper or my model? Lord, perhaps You have given me Ruby to remind me that You provide the help I need to accomplish whatever task You set me to. If You want me to feed Your sheep, I must trust that You will open the way. If you want me to do it through financial gifts, You will provide the source of income. If You want me to do it through the dogs, You will show me the way. I just need to trust and open my soul to Your generosity, so that I may open myself to Your work, in whatever form it may take.

Trust

A father catches his gleeful child,
Whom he has playfully tossed into the air.
It's a matter of trust.
So I need to put my total trust in You,
Abba, Almighty Father.
I need to trust that You will always be there to catch me.
You are the one who watches over me, all day, every day.
Teach me to place my total trust in You.
Too often, I squirm away from your leading,
Certain that everything is my own responsibility.
I am consumed with guilt
Over every little detail.
I fail to give You credit
For the good
And for that which goes awry of my own planning.
I fail to believe that
For everything, there is a season.
I fail to trust.
Lord, Abba,
Teach me to trust.
Teach me to rest my whole self in Your hands.

Amen.

CHAPTER FIFTEEN

Total Surrender

MacKenzie comes to me in a dream. Joyfully, I greet him, hug him, and tell him how much I've loved him and missed him. But something nags at me. MacKenzie is dead. According to the popular mythos, he should be waiting for me at the Rainbow Bridge, ready to help me across when my time comes. Does his presence here and now mean my time has come? I do a quick self-evaluation of my physical being. I grimly recognize that all is not as it should be. My heart is laboring, and my breathing is strained. Perhaps it is my time. Frantically, I call to God. No! I mentally scream, *Not yet! I'm not ready to leave this world! I don't want to die, Not yet!*

A cold, dark silence is my only answer.

Jesus? Are you there? You promised to be here for me. You promised that I only had to reach out for you. Well, I'm reaching. Are You there? Please, I don't want to die! Please, not yet!

But there is no answering reassurance. Sobbing inside, I know what I have to do, oh me of so little faith. I have to let go of self, totally surrender to His will if I expect Him to help me now. I have to die to self. Am I really willing to surrender myself to Him, even if it means my death?

Oh, Lord, this is hard, I cry. I don't want to die now. I'm afraid, Lord. I'm afraid to let go of self; I'm afraid to die." Still, I know it is what I must do. Gulping back my terror, I whimper in a weak, pitiful voice. "Lord, I accept. I put my trust in You. If it is Your will that my life ends here and now, so be it. I am Yours."

Silence is my only answer.

"Lord," I plea in a stronger voice; "You are my Savior. In You, I put my entire self. Into Your hands, I put my keeping. Do as You will with me." I am still terribly frightened, but I am sincere. Then, instead of being cold and empty, the darkness and silence feel warm and soothing. I know He has accepted me, and that it is not yet time for me to leave this life.

I sleep.

In the morning, as I once again take up my daily responsibilities, I think about MacKenzie, Ruby, and all of the dogs of the past and present. My old dogs trusted me with their lives and with their deaths. It has been my honor, my decision to be with each one as their end time came. Some crossed over without assistance, but others I held while the vet did his deadly deed. And yes, I cried, even knowing in my heart that this was what had to be. When Ruby's time comes, I will again have to choose to either let her pain and suffering on earth continue or to give her freedom in the next world. While I am only human and don't have all the answers, I do have a level of knowledge and foreseeing that she doesn't. But being Ruby, she likely will lie quietly in my arms and accept. Last night, I learned that I, too, can lie quietly in the arms of my Lord and accept whatever it is He has planned for me. It isn't necessarily easy, but I can do it. I can completely turn myself over to Him, trusting even to the point of death.

A Prayer of Surrender

Dear Lord, my heavenly Father,
You have blessed me
And ask so little in exchange.
Yet, at the same time, You ask for everything.
You gave me free will, but You ask in return that
I surrender it to You.
I ponder if that which makes me unique will still exist
If I so completely turn myself over to You.
What is free will; what is self, if I don't exercise it?
Would I be me if I didn't take charge of myself?
Or would I be only an extension of another?
How can I still be me if I die to self?
Who will I be if I surrender myself to You?
Will I become a piece of You?
Or will You become a piece of me?
In your endless wisdom,
You can guide me in my life's decisions.
You don't ask much of me—You only ask me to listen
and to heed You.
So I ask You to guide me in this decision.
Help me to understand what You mean by dying to self,
what it is that You really want.
Be with me, Father, and help me, guide me,
in my blindness.

Amen.

CHAPTER SIXTEEN

The Body and Blood of Christ

Ruby is at the kennel gate, staring at me intently. I think she has another message for me. I gaze back into her eyes, trying to decipher what she has to say. Her canine voice reaches into my heart and demands to be heard. But it isn't Ruby I hear; it is the voice of Jesus telling me who I am, who I am meant to be.

"YOU are my body and blood, my Eucharist."

The thought is startling, to say the least. In fact, it's downright appalling. *Seriously, Jesus, do you really mean me? Couldn't be!* Yet it is true. I have opened myself up to Him, have died to self (in theory, at least) and have asked Him to replace me with His own being, if you will. I have partaken in communion and incorporated His body and blood as building blocks in my own spiritual growth. Now, after a lifetime of feeling as if I'm on ice, He calls me out, declaring, "You are now My body and blood. It is upon you to feed and nourish My people."

OK, Jesus, so I really AM your body and blood. You must know that the very thought leaves me scared, downright terrified!

How do you expect me to do this? Isn't it arrogant of me to claim this title, this role?

"No, it's not." He assures me. "It is a part of My Truth."

Sure, I'm hardly the only one with this claim, I protest.

Again, God assures me. "Regardless of who else I may call, it doesn't change the fact that you belong to My family."

I am the BODY and blood of Christ. Perhaps all who come to live in Christ are His body and blood. The Church has accepted the claim of being His body, and I am a part of the Church. I have been active in various roles—lector, parish council, Eucharistic minister. Our parish has been notable for our ownership of the parish. It isn't hard to see that as a part of the active parish community, I am, indeed the body of Christ. While I am not the only one called, is it so hard to see that He asks me to act as His eyes, ears, hands, and legs, even His voice at times? Is it that hard to see that I must take one more step up and nourish the Church, not just be nourished by it?

I am the body and BLOOD of Christ. Why do I resist, hold back? It is said that Siberian Huskies are remarkable in that they give so fully of themselves, but always hold something back. Some feel it is a preservation thing. But I don't want to preserve myself. I want to give ALL to Christ. At least, I have tried to convince myself of that. Now here I face that ultimate question, can I give entirely of myself, even to the point of my lifeblood? I shudder deep inside at the request God has made. Why do I find it so hard to engage myself fully in Christ? I take a deep breath and pray.

Dear Lord, You are asking so much of me. Part of me wants to be like a Siberian, to hold back that last little bit. Yet, You did not hold back. You gave Your very own son to us sinners. And He did not hold back. He did not relish the ordeal before Him when He prayed in Gethsemane, but He still gave himself over to death. Yes, I fear what this sacrifice, this Blood entails. But here I stand, Lord, before You. Here I pledge to accept Your gift of Blood, Your transfusion of support. I accept the mission You have put before me, to be Your body and blood.

What does Ruby have to say about all this? I look into her laughing eyes and see my answer. "It's about time, Mom. You finally see the truth."

"Ruby, I may have had my eyes opened at last, but I still need you. I need all the guidance I can garner. You have been a channel between God and me. Now, more than ever, I need that channel wide open."

Thank You, dear Father, for Ruby. Thank You for opening my eyes, my heart, and my soul. You have blessed me; You have filled me with Your spirit and given me Your peace. I am the body and blood of Christ. It is now my time to step forward, so I mentally gird my loins and move forward, ever under Your guidance and protection. Shalom.

A Prayer for Completion

Driven by a fervor,
I sought You, O Lord.
I wanted to be near You, every day, all day.
I ached for Your presence in my life, in me.
Your love for me has overwhelmed me.
Now in return, I just want to open myself to You.
You complete me.
To be without You is to have a part of me missing.
I cannot live without You, Lord.
Come. I welcome You to me.
Make me a part of Your flock.
Make me over.
You are a part of me—make me a part of You.
Do not set aside this burning, aching, yearning of mine,
O Lord.
Fulfill it.

Amen.

About the Author

Linda was raised in Colorado, where the mountains helped shape her early life. While in college, she converted to Catholicism and later married her high school sweetheart, Bob, a member the US Army. She followed him to Germany, and over the next twenty years, they raised five children in four different  countries and nine states. Today, they live in a rural, wooded area in upstate New York. Linda returned to college, where she received her B.S. degree from Cornell University. Linda and Bob are active members at Our Lady of Perpetual Help, a Catholic mission church, but also enjoy visiting their children and many grandchildren. Although her racing days are over, she still enjoys working with her Siberian Huskies. Along with writing memoirs, devotions, and children's stories, she is an award-winning photographer. Linda has had numerous articles published at FaithWriters.com, her local paper, and the Siberian Quarterly. God has used her dogs to help her become closer to Jesus, and she is excited to share these epiphanies with others.

CPSIA information can be obtained
at www.ICGtesting.com
Printed in the USA
FFOW04n1930211017
41393FF

Me, Ruby, and God

I hope you enjoyed this small book about Ruby
and how she taught me about a loving God.
It has been a privilege to share our story with you.

This book is available at a special low cost
for quantity purchases. Please visit my website,
GoldenRubyPublishing.com to discover how you can share
this book with others while earning money for your group
or organization.

May God bless you with a renewed understanding
of the Father's love
and a heart that knows His peace.

Linda Crowley